FASHIONED to Reign

Other Books and Materials by Kris Vallotton

Developing a Supernatural Lifestyle:
A Practical Guide to a Life of Signs, Wonders, and Miracles

God's Most Beautiful Creation
(a six-part DVD or CD teaching series on women)

Heavy Rain: Renew the Church,
Transform the World

Moral Revolution:
The Naked Truth about Sexual Purity

Outrageous Courage:
What God Can Do with Raw Obedience and Radical Faith
(the Tracy Evans story; co-authored with Jason Vallotton)

School of the Prophets:
Advanced Training for Prophetic Ministry
(book, workbook, leader's guide and video segments available,
or an all-inclusive curriculum kit)

Spirit Wars:
Winning the Invisible Battle against Sin and the Enemy
(book, workbook, leader's guide and video segments available
individually, or as an all-inclusive curriculum kit)

The Supernatural Power of Forgiveness:
Discover How to Escape Your Prison of Pain and Unlock a Life of Freedom
(co-authored with Jason Vallotton)

The Supernatural Ways of Royalty:
Discovering Your Rights and Privileges of Being a Son or Daughter of God
(co-authored with Bill Johnson)

Basic Training for the Supernatural Ways of Royalty
(workbook)

Basic Training for the Prophetic Ministry
(workbook)

FASHIONED to Reign

Empowering Women
to Fulfill Their Divine Destiny

KRIS VALLOTTON

Chosen

a division of Baker Publishing Group
Minneapolis, Minnesota

Published by Chosen Books
11400 Hampshire Avenue South
Bloomington, Minnesota 55438
www.chosenbooks.com

Chosen Books is a division of
Baker Publishing Group, Grand Rapids, Michigan

Printed in the United States of America

ISBN 978-0-8007-9607-5 (pbk.)

Cover design by Dan Pitts

14 15 16 17 18 19 20   7 6 5 4 3 2 1

Contents

Launching a *Fashioned to Reign* Group   7

Preparing to Lead   11

Formatting Your Group Sessions   16

Checklist for Leaders   19

Session 1 Guide: "Fashioned" by God   21

Session 2 Guide: Unmasking the Devil   28

Session 3 Guide: Standing for the Word   33

Session 4 Guide: The First Women's Lib Movement   37

Session 5 Guide: Just a Misunderstanding   42

Session 6 Guide: A Careful Excavation   46

Session 7 Guide: Role Reversals   50

Session 8 Guide: Powerful Diversity   55

Optional Final Meeting: *Fashioned to Reign* Celebration   60

Launching a
Fashioned to Reign Group

Once you have decided to launch a group study of *Fashioned to Reign*, you can approach it in a number of ways. Whatever approach you choose, I trust the end result will be the same—a revolutionized understanding of God's purposes in fashioning women. I trust you will also gain a new appreciation for the role God has destined His daughters to play in co-reigning alongside His sons with grace, intuition and compassion to help nurture this ailing world back to health.

The *Fashioned to Reign Curriculum Kit* contains everything you need to make those end results a reality, with one exception. You and your group members will need that power from on high Jesus talked about when He told His disciples, "You will receive power when the Holy Spirit has come upon you; and you shall be My witnesses both in Jerusalem, and in all Judea and Samaria, and even to the remotest part of the earth" (Acts 1:8). To embrace and extend the good news of how God has fashioned, gifted and called women, you will need the presence of the Holy Spirit in attendance at your group meetings. Make sure to invite Him in and give Him room to work in you and through you as you lead your group through this *Fashioned to Reign* study.

Let's take a look at the different ways you could launch and lead a *Fashioned to Reign* study. As you choose an approach and formulate a plan, consider your situation, seek the Lord's direction, take stock of the resources you have available and ask Him for His creativity.

Church Life Group or Small Group Approach

Many churches offer life groups or small groups that meet regularly outside the church, usually in someone's home. Such a group provides an ideal setting in which to study *Fashioned to Reign.* Your church may already have such groups in place. If not, you may want to suggest forming them, at least temporarily, for the purpose of this study. Each group would meet for eight or nine sessions (usually once a week) specifically to focus on the material presented in *Fashioned to Reign.*

Each group that forms should include at least four or five people to facilitate discussion, with a maximum of ten or twelve people. Groups larger than a dozen make it difficult for everyone to give input and receive feedback effectively. Larger groups can divide into more numerous, smaller groups or move toward a church class approach (which I will discuss next). Here are the essentials for leading a group study:

- A consistent meeting place, either in the leader's home, another home or a space the church provides.
- Adequate technology in the form of a DVD player/TV/computer large enough and loud enough for all the group members to see and hear. (A small laptop playing at the far end of a room may make it difficult for a dozen people to get the most out of the teachings.)
- A committed leader/facilitator who is familiar with the material ahead of time and who is willing to follow the lead of the Holy Spirit as the group moves through the teachings. This could be an individual, or it could be a team, perhaps husband/wife hosts or two church leaders working together. The leader(s) will direct the sessions from beginning to end and perhaps call group members or send them online reminders about the meetings.
- A plan or schedule for the group meetings to keep them flowing through the various elements that will occupy the group's time together—fellowship, worship, prayer, a video teaching, discussion and ministry time. (Two sections ahead, in "Formatting Your Group Sessions," I provide a sample schedule that I think will work well for group meetings.)

Once you have these leadership essentials in place, you are ready to set a date for your first session and sign people up to take part in your group.

Church Class/Midweek Meeting/ Sunday School Approach

In addition to weekend services, most churches offer some kind of church classes to disciple members and help them grow. These classes often cover a wide variety of topics that change from time to time, and meeting times may range from midweek services to Sunday school classes to some other agreed-upon time like a Saturday morning Bible study. Any of these models could lend itself to a study of *Fashioned to Reign.*

Since a large number of people are usually involved in such classes, the discussion element of a *Fashioned to Reign* study (or any other study) may become more of a challenge than it would be in a smaller group, but leaders can still encourage some dialogue. Also, because of time constraints, it may be necessary to extend the number of weeks to allow sufficient time for the class to work its way through the study. For example, a class could take two weeks to cover each session. One week could be devoted to watching a video segment for a particular session of the *Fashioned to Reign* study and talking about the principles I present in the video and in the book readings. The following week could be devoted to class discussion of the questions and life applications involved in that session.

Although small groups are an ideal approach to this study and are the model I had in mind as I put together this curriculum kit, you can certainly adapt a class approach as an effective model to get these principles across to a larger group already accustomed to meeting at a regular time. The ability to increase our understanding of God's plans and purposes for His beautiful daughters does not change based on the size of the group or the setting. If you will give the Holy Spirit room to work, you can effectively teach *Fashioned to Reign* in a variety of settings. Do not feel that the effects of this study will be limited if you need to adopt more of a classroom approach.

Church-Wide Group Study Approach

In this approach, the pastor and senior leadership of a church decide to take the entire church through a study of *Fashioned to Reign* together. Weekend sermons would focus on the principles presented in the book and video segments (and some video clips might be shown in services). Sunday school/midweek classes/small groups would all focus on some aspect of the study, perhaps watching the video teachings together and discussing the questions and life applications.

The church-wide approach could be presented as *40 Days of Fashioned to Reign* (reflecting the eight sessions of five daily studies each in the workbook). Each congregant could be encouraged to make the most of the church-wide focus by reading the *Fashioned to Reign* book, going through the workbook and participating in group sessions.

This approach is a great way to get everyone in a church body moving in the same direction, toward acknowledging that women are as qualified, called and gifted as men and toward empowering them to fulfill their divine destinies. It is especially effective if a small group component is added to the overall church focus.

Individual Study Approach

As I said, I had group studies in mind when I designed this kit. Where there is no group study or church focus available to take part in, however, individuals can use the *Fashioned to Reign* book, workbook and video segments on their own to excavate the Scriptures with me concerning women and their role in the Church and to gain a clearer understanding of what God intended that role to be.

With the Holy Spirit as teacher and guide in an individual study of these materials, a person can learn from the Scriptures how women of the past lived powerfully and what a strong advocate women found in Jesus when He walked the earth. (I believe He is still their most powerful advocate today.) Again, the Holy Spirit's effectiveness is not limited to a certain size group or a certain setting. But if there is a group study to join, I do recommend that approach because of the fellowship, encouragement and discussion opportunities such a group can provide.

Preparing to Lead

While format should never replace flexibility when it comes to following the lead of the Holy Spirit, in a group setting the presence of the Lord is stewarded best in the midst of organization. Someone has to oversee the practical preparations for a group study, watch over the time schedule, facilitate the flow of the meeting and the ministry and pray for the group ahead of time. That someone will be you as the group leader or class facilitator. Let me give you some guidelines that will help you prepare to lead this study and minister to the participants.

Prepare with Prayer

I am sure it goes without saying that your first step in preparing to lead a *Fashioned to Reign* group is prayer. You have already prayed for the Lord's direction and determined that you are supposed to lead a group through this study. Continue to pray for increased insight on your part into the ability and call of women to lead both in society and in the Church, and pray for a deeper understanding of the spiritual principles you will be covering as you lead the group. Spend some time with the Holy Spirit, asking Him to give you vision for what this study can accomplish in your life and the lives of the participants.

Session by session, pray for your group or class meetings ahead of time, and pray for the individuals who will attend. Be ready and willing to entertain questions, and be patient and persistent as you guide the group through these materials. For many, the concept of women co-reigning with men and leading in the Church will be new—or quite possibly the complete opposite of what they have been taught through the misapplication of some Scriptures we will examine in detail. The Lord is about to do a marvelous work in the life of each person in your group, whether male or female, as you walk through these sessions together.

Prepare with Study

Prepare to lead your *Fashioned to Reign* group by studying the material ahead of time yourself. Your first exposure to the principles contained in *Fashioned to Reign* should not take place in the middle of leading your group. By the time you meet for a session, you should have already read the assigned Scripture and book readings, watched the video segment, tackled the "Questions to Consider" yourself and made some life application in your daily walk.

In fact, I think it is a wise idea to work through the entire curriculum in this kit before taking on a leadership role, so that you are familiar with what is coming in each of the sessions. That will better prepare you to answer questions that may arise or direct the group to put a certain topic on hold until you reach the particular session that covers it. You will gain confidence and assurance to lead when you study ahead of time so that you will know where you are going with the group and how you will get there.

You do not need to be a brilliant academic scholar or hermeneutical expert to understand the material I present in *Fashioned to Reign*. While I was extremely careful with the scriptural scholarship required to put these truths on the printed page, they are truths understood more with the spirit than with the mind. Nonetheless, a little diligent scholarship can go a long way toward increasing the net spiritual effect of a study like this. As Jesus told us in Luke 6:39–40, "A blind man cannot guide a blind man, can he? Will they not both fall into a pit? A pupil is not above his teacher; but everyone, after he has been fully trained, will be like his teacher." If you will be diligent in your study to search out the truths contained in *Fashioned to Reign*, your group participants will see your familiarity with the material and the skill with which you handle it, and it will motivate them to be like you.

Prepare on a Practical Level

You have probably heard the saying that some Christians are so heavenly minded that they are no earthly good. It is true that you cannot wage war or take much territory for the Kingdom of God if you are so focused on heaven that you cannot walk out your faith powerfully while you are here on earth.

In other words, in addition to your preparation time in prayer and study, you need to prepare to lead on a practical level. If you will attend to the practical details, things will go much more smoothly in your group.

After you know which approach you are using, determine a meeting location that has sufficient space for your group and appropriate audio-visual equipment to play the video segments. The more comfortable you can make the setting, the more people will look forward to the meetings, without being distracted by issues like not enough seating or inadequate, uncooperative equipment. When you take care of the practical things ahead of time, you minimize distractions and give yourself credibility as a leader.

Once the place is all ready, set a schedule for your meetings. Pick a time period when your church calendar is not already filled with special events that will require large amounts of people's time. They will be more apt to commit to your group when they are not overcommitted in other areas. Check with other church leadership and the pastor(s) to make sure your proposed study does not conflict with anything major on the agenda, and then set a starting date. You should plan to follow the eight-session curriculum (or nine) consistently and consecutively to make the best use of your group's time together.

Once you establish a time period for your study, pick a day of the week and a time to meet (unless those are already determined in a church class or the like). It can be hard to accommodate everyone's work and home life schedules, but choose a day and time that will work best for the majority. Perhaps you can consider offering an alternate study at a future date for those unable to attend your current group.

Decide ahead of time about other practical matters such as whether your group will include refreshments or will make provision for childcare. Again, planning ahead in these areas can eliminate a host of distractions once your group begins. (I talk more about the specifics of planning your group time together in the section just ahead.)

Prepare to Get the Word Out

For a church-connected group study to succeed, church leadership must endorse it. Make sure your pastor and church leaders are aware of your proposed *Fashioned to Reign* study and are behind it. They can position themselves to help you with the launch by getting the word out.

Use multiple means, if possible, to let people at your church know a study group is forming and that they are invited to participate. See if an announcement can be made from the pulpit. Advertise the group on your church's website. Post a sign-up sheet and print flyers. Send out emails and post the event on your church's social media outlets. Make personal phone calls to individuals you sense should be involved in your group.

Prepare Potential Co-leaders or Assistants

Often, there will be people right in your group who are good candidates for co-leaders or assistants, and you may need them. Once you have a list of participant names, prayerfully consider whether there is someone on the list who is spiritually solid and mature, who could back you up during group ministry time or take your place leading the group in the event that you must miss a session.

Also think about names on the list who could assist with the practical side of things. Is there someone who enjoys working in the kitchen? Could that person oversee refreshments session to session or circulate a sign-up sheet so that you would not have to? Is there someone who enjoys children? Would that person be willing to plan activities for the group's children or make sure to enlist teens or other helpers to come in and do childcare for the couple hours that you meet? Is there someone on the list who enjoys showing hospitality? Might that person open his or her home to the group meetings and take care of the physical environment for you so that you can attend to the spiritual atmosphere?

You do not need to do everything yourself to lead a successful group. In fact, it might be better if you did not! Let the participants invest in the group by contributing to its welfare. There may be some who simply want to come, listen and learn, and go home, but others will be more than willing to help out if asked. They may even offer before you ask. Take them up on it!

Prepare Your Participants

As participants sign up for your group, let them know what they are getting into, so to speak. It might be a good idea to print out an information sheet that participants can take home as soon as they sign up. Listed on that sheet should be the time, place and dates of your sessions, along with the materials everyone involved in the group will need. Participants should each have a copy of *Fashioned to Reign* and the *Fashioned to Reign Workbook*. They will not need the leader's guide or the video segments/DVDs unless they plan to lead a group in the future. You, however, will need both to lead the group. You can purchase all the necessary materials together in one place in the *Fashioned to Reign Leader's Kit*.

If your church has a bookstore, inquire about whether it can stock the *Fashioned to Reign* materials during the course of your group study (and beyond). You could also make the materials available for purchase at your sign-up table, or at least have copies on hand for participants to look at so they can find and order the book and workbook online.

If you are able, it might also be good to have a few extra copies of both the book and workbook available for purchase at your first meeting, in case any latecomers join in and still need the materials. Your group will get off to a good start if you let everyone know how to obtain the *Fashioned to Reign* book and workbook quickly and easily so that they can get started with the study.

As they sign up, also let the participants know that *before* the group starts, they should work through Session 1 in the workbook, which includes readings from the book and from Scripture. That way, everyone will be on the same page and you can jump right in at that first meeting. The participants would then continue to work through one session per meeting *prior* to each meeting. You could even consider including a syllabus on the information sheet that you hand out so that everyone can easily stay on schedule.

Formatting Your Group Sessions

*A*s I said in the preparation section, format should not replace flexibility. It should, however, provide a foundation from which ministry can flow. If you have a dozen people in your *Fashioned to Reign* group and no format planned for your meetings, you will be pulled in a dozen different directions. As the group leader, it is your responsibility to come with a plan in hand, ready to direct the group. You may be led to follow the plan to the letter in all your meetings, or in some sessions the Holy Spirit may lead you in another direction. Either of those is fine, as long as you are prepared to start with a plan.

Several different elements can make up a group study. Some are necessary to this *Fashioned to Reign* study, while others are optional. The necessary elements are an introduction and opening prayer, time to watch the video segment, group discussion in which you talk about the video guide and the discussion questions, a "Life Application" review and group announcements about what to do to prepare for the next meeting. The optional elements are a time of worship, a fellowship/refreshments time and a group ministry time.

Pray and think through these elements, and then format a meeting schedule that incorporates the ones you will include. What follows is a sample schedule for an evening meeting that includes a few optional elements, along with the necessary ones. You can add or subtract from this sample schedule, adjusting it as needed to fit your group.

Sample Schedule: *Fashioned to Reign* Group Evening Meeting

- 6:15 Leader(s) arrive at meeting place (a home or other location) to connect with hosts/co-leaders/assistants. Make sure as leadership that you arrive on time. If you run late or come unprepared, your group members will sense the stress when they arrive. Frazzled, last-minute preparations put everyone on edge and prohibit a sense of peace and readiness. You will set an atmosphere for powerful ministry right from the start by being on time and coming well prepared for the evening.

- 6:15–6:30 Test all AV equipment for video viewing and/or worship to make sure everything is functioning properly. Have a backup plan in case of any malfunctions. Check on refreshments and childcare arrangements, if applicable. Review the evening's schedule with any assistants.

- 6:30–6:40 Pray together for the evening ahead. Possible prayer directives: for the Holy Spirit to move and minister freely; for the teaching to connect with and bring truth to all who hear it; for sensitivity to the Lord's direction in the leader(s); for conversation and discussion that edifies; for transparency and a close bond among group members; for life application of the lessons learned; for testimonies of the power of God at work through this study.

- 6:40–7:10 Do a final check to make sure you and your location are ready for the evening. Welcome group members as they arrive. Direct them to refreshments if those are provided, and make sure everyone has a comfortable spot. This is a good time to encourage fellowship among group members.

- 7:10–7:20 Gather everyone together. Have them bring their books and workbooks and prepare to get started. Welcome the group and briefly review with them which session and topics the meeting will cover. Pray for the evening aloud, or ask a group member to do so.

- 7:20–7:30 Worship time. Have someone lead a couple of worship songs as you welcome the presence of the Lord at your meeting.

- 7:30–7:50 View the video segment applicable to the session you are covering. Suggest that group members fill in the video guide in their workbook as they watch.

- 7:50–8:20 Discussion time. Briefly comment on the video segment and give the answers to the video guide, then cover the session questions contained in this leader's guide. Read the session questions aloud one by one (since the participant workbooks do not contain them), and ask group members for their comments. If time allows, also ask participants if there was anything in the session or the book itself that leapt out at them. Were there any ideas they struggled with? Anything that brought new understanding of a Scripture they had previously misunderstood? Engage in dialogue as a group to process this session's principles together.

- 8:20–8:30 Go over the "Life Application" section from the workbook and allow for a couple testimonies of what group members did as application and what resulted from their efforts. This important part of the *Fashioned to Reign* study brings the lessons home and helps group members apply them to daily life.

- 8:30 Bring the meeting to a close by reviewing which workbook session group members should work through in preparation for the next meeting. Offer a closing prayer and an opportunity for ministry to take place, if time allows. You could invite group members who want prayer to stay, and dismiss the rest.

Checklist for Leaders

One or Two Months Ahead

☐ Have you determined the approach that is best suited for you to use for your *Fashioned to Reigns* study? (If not, see the section titled "Launching a *Fashioned to Reign* Group.")

☐ Have you determined a start and end date for your session meetings and checked your church calendar for possible conflicts? Have you picked a day and time that will allow for the most participation?

☐ Have you secured a meeting location that will accommodate your projected group size and that has proper AV equipment?

☐ Have you begun to advertise the *Fashioned to Reign* group study through your church, available social media and the like? Do you have a sign-up sheet ready?

☐ Have you determined how and where to purchase materials and ordered your *Fashioned to Reign Leader's Kit*? Do you have purchasing information ready for participants, who will need to buy or order their *Fashioned to Reign* book and *Fashioned to Reign Workbook* ahead of time?

☐ Have you put together an information sheet to hand out to people who sign up for your group? It should list the meeting dates, time and location, as well as the materials group members will need and where they can get them.

Two to Four Weeks Ahead

☐ Do you have your *Fashioned to Reign Leader's Kit* in hand? Are you going through the material to familiarize yourself with it prior to leading the group study?

☐ Have you read over the sample meeting schedule in the previous section, "Formatting Your Group Sessions," and adjusted it to fit the group you will lead?

☐ If your meeting schedule will include elements such as worship or fellowship with refreshments, have you considered finding an assistant to help you oversee those areas?

☐ Have you considered enlisting a co-leader, a spiritually mature believer who can help you in each session during ministry/prayer time and possibly lead a group meeting in the event of your absence?

One Week Ahead

☐ Have you contacted those who signed up for your group to make sure they remember the starting date/time and are ready to begin?

☐ Have you asked your participants if they have purchased the *Fashioned to Reign* book and workbook? Have you reminded them to go through Session 1 in preparation for your group's first meeting?

☐ Have you double-checked all your AV equipment to make sure everything is in working order? Do you have a backup plan in place in case anything malfunctions?

One or Two Days Ahead

☐ Have you reviewed Session 1 in the leader's guide, book and workbook so you are ready to handle questions and comments from the group? (It would be wise to review each session a day or two prior to your meetings.)

☐ Have you contacted any assistants who are overseeing worship/refreshments/childcare to make sure they have everything in place?

☐ Have you gathered your materials together so you are ready to walk out the door on time on the first meeting day?

First Meeting Day

☐ Have you allowed yourself sufficient time to arrive at your meeting location early?

☐ Have you looked over your meeting schedule again so you have the order of events in mind? (Keep in mind that the flow of ministry is facilitated by organization.)

☐ Have you put on the full armor of God today? Then you are ready to go forth in power to help women of God in your group, in your church, in your family and in your community realize their full potential, purpose and power in Christ.

Session 1 Guide

"Fashioned" by God

*I*n the following pages, I provide you with a step-by-step guide for each session to help you facilitate your group meetings. You can follow this guide, just as it is written, to take your group from start to finish as you go through the curriculum. If the Holy Spirit directs you to spend more time on one element and less on another, however, or to rearrange the elements in a certain meeting, by all means follow His lead! But again, planning a format for your meetings ahead of time gives you a solid foundation from which ministry can flow. These session guides provide you with that foundation.

This Session 1 guide gives more detailed instructions than the other session guides that follow because it sets the tone for the rest of your meetings. You can refer back to it from session to session, as needed, to refresh your memory about how to navigate through the different elements of your group time together efficiently. But each session guide repeats the basic elements and time allotments for you.

In each of these session guides, I provide the answers to the fill-in-the-blank video guide participants will fill out in their workbooks as they watch the video segment. I also provide session discussion questions that I hope will encourage lively group dialogue. While the session discussion questions are not included in the participant workbooks, they are based both on the video segment and on the workbook's daily "Questions to Consider," which participants have already answered in preparation for your meeting.

In brief, Session 1 covers material from the Introduction and chapters 1 and 2 of *Fashioned to Reign*, along with the Session 1 pages from the participant workbook. In this session, I talk about how desperately we need matriarchs to step up alongside patriarchs in every area of society and the Church. I also cover the Genesis story of creation from a new and unique perspective—Adam's point of view. Then we talk about how we all, male and female, were created "after the God kind," and what that might have meant, exactly, if Adam and Eve were two halves of a whole. (I know that sounds strange, but stay with me. It is just one possibility I discuss.) I also talk a little bit about being single yet whole, and give the example of Mother Teresa as a single woman who accomplished more in her life and ministry than most of us ever dream of.

Leadership Prayer Focus (before the meeting): Ask the Lord to give your participants an awareness of the need for matriarchs to step up into their rightful places next to patriarchs in both society and the Church, but especially in the Church. Ask that participants would, through the narrative story of Adam, catch a glimpse of the glory of creation and the beauty of the way God "fashioned" the first woman. Also pray that any singles in your group would understand their wholeness through the Holy Spirit.

Welcome and Fellowship Time (20–30 minutes): You should be ready 20 minutes before your meeting begins to start welcoming participants. Try to connect with each person as he or she enters the meeting place. Greet people, introduce them to others whom they may not know and direct them to enjoy some fellowship (and refreshments if applicable) until the group begins. Connectedness is important, and it starts with you as the leader. Many people attend small groups or church classes to learn and grow, but they miss out on making connections with other believers. You can help facilitate those connections by being available at the beginning of each session to greet participants as they arrive and introduce them to each other.

This would also be a good time to check with participants as they come in about whether they have the *Fashioned to Reign* book and workbook. Ideally, they will have purchased their materials and worked through Session 1 before this first meeting. That may not be the case for late sign-ups or some others, though. Try to have a few copies of both the book and the workbook available for purchase at your meetings so that everyone can follow along as you go through the materials.

Gather and Begin (10 minutes): Gather everyone together into the actual meeting area, inviting them to bring along their books, workbooks and something to write with. This first session (and any other sessions where there are newcomers), introduce yourself and outline the purpose of the group—to study *Fashioned to Reign* together and learn about the way God fashioned, called and equipped women to co-reign alongside men.

As an icebreaker, allow participants to briefly give their names and perhaps one interesting fact about themselves. (You can decide whether to do this only at the first meeting, or at every meeting.) Then discuss the meeting schedule with your group and briefly overview what your group sessions will look like. Make sure to mention that you will cover one session per meeting in the group, and that participants should read the materials and do the workbook pages for that session *prior* to the meetings.

Also take a few minutes at this first meeting to briefly orient participants to the book and workbook. (You can do this privately with newcomers at future sessions.) If you gave clear instruction about how to use the materials when people signed up to attend, most of them will have worked through Session 1 already and will be familiar with the curriculum. Mention, however, that as they work through the curriculum in preparation for each group meeting, the study involved will require a time commitment of 15–20 minutes per day (five days of readings and accompanying workbook pages per session). Encourage everyone to fully engage with the curriculum since they will get out of it as much as they put into it. The purpose for the daily assignments is not to add busywork to already busy schedules, but to cultivate a habit of Bible study and daily time in the presence of God as participants seek to understand the God-ordained role of women in the Church and in the earth. Assure them that the results will be more than worth their time and effort!

If you are including an optional ninth session at which you plan to engage in some sort of social activity or have a meal together, you may want to mention that added session now so that everyone will realize that the curriculum materials will run for the first eight sessions, with the final ninth session being dedicated to wrap-up and fellowship.

Opening Prayer, Worship (10 minutes): Each session, pray for the meeting aloud, specifically addressing the topic you will be covering in your time together. Or you can ask a group member to pray aloud.

If your group includes a worship element, this time early in the meeting is a good place for worship since it stirs a hunger in people for God's presence and prepares their hearts to hear what the Holy Spirit has to teach them. If you or another group member can lead a few worship songs on an instrument or with your voice, that is wonderful. You can also worship with a CD or DVD, but make sure you have tested it and set it to the songs you have chosen ahead of time so that your transition into worship goes smoothly. (Technical difficulties can be a huge distraction to the flow of worship.) Or your group can sing a couple songs a cappella. The method of worship is not as important as the goal, which is to refresh believers in God's presence and draw them close to Him and to each other as your group meeting begins.

After worship opens the door, the atmosphere is typically charged with God's presence. It is not unusual for people to receive words of knowledge, wisdom or prophetic words in that atmosphere, or to experience other manifestations of the Holy Spirit. A group study such as this one is a great place in which people can "practice" these gifts and minister to each other. A word of caution, though: As group leader, it is up to you to steward your participants' time well. That means monitoring your group for distractions or disorder. Watch for people who might want to take charge of prayer or worship time inappropriately and distract from the order of the evening. Once you sense that the Holy Spirit is ready for the group to move on, interject that those who wish to do so can come back to more prayer time at the end of the meeting, but that for now, you need to move on with the meeting schedule as planned.

Also watch for people who might seek to monopolize the group's time with their problems or who have issues requiring more specialized counsel than your group setting allows. Gently direct them to put their comments on hold and talk to you after the group study part of the meeting is concluded. Stress that it is important for the group as a whole to move through the materials as scheduled so that everyone present can get the most from the curriculum, but that you will come back to their concerns at a later point. At the end of the meeting, after the group has been dismissed, you can minister to such people in prayer or direct them to an appropriate counselor in the church who can help them further.

Video Teaching (20–30 minutes): At this point, transition into teaching time by having the group watch the video segment that goes along with Session 1. In it, I will touch on some topics the book has already covered, and I will also present some new insights into the material. Participants should have workbooks and pens in hand so they can fill in the video guide in the workbook as they watch and listen. In each video segment, I will give them all the information they need to fill in the blanks on the accompanying workbook page. Again, make sure to test and set up all AV equipment *prior* to your meetings so that when you push *PLAY*, the video plays without a hitch. Preparation is key when it comes to AV.

Here are the answers for the Session 1 video guide. Take a minute to review these answers with your group after the video so they can fill in any blanks they missed.

1. When God made Adam, He made him both <u>male</u> and <u>female</u>. And they were made in His <u>image</u> and in His <u>likeness</u>.

2. If you <u>oppress</u> women, you lose half the <u>revelation</u> of the nature of God.

3. It takes both male and female to <u>represent</u> the Godhead.

4. The word *rib* in Scripture actually is the word <u>side</u> <u>chamber</u>.

5. God took a rib from Adam, and He <u>fashioned</u> that rib.

6. God <u>formed</u> man (and animals) from dirt, but He <u>fashioned</u> woman from more sophisticated material (the rib).

Discussion/Dialogue Time (30–40 minutes): Now it is time to get your group members dialoguing about the things they are learning in this session. Open up the dialogue with the following discussion questions. Some questions are new, from the fresh ideas I presented in the video segment. Others revisit some of the questions I asked in the daily workbook pages for this session, so that participants have a chance to talk over their workbook answers and gain insight from each other. If there are Scriptures connected to a particular question, encourage participation by asking a group member to read the Scripture aloud. Then read the discussion question to the group and ask for input. Given the topics we cover in this *Fashioned to Reign* study, I do not think it will take long before you have a lively discussion going in every session meeting.

—— *Session 1 Discussion Questions* ——————

1. Kris mentioned in today's video that the Adam narrative he wrote in his journal is historical fiction in that although he tried to stay within boundaries of Scripture, he filled in the spaces by using his imagination and tried to give the story color. What did you think of his "imagineering"? Can you see some of the story happening in the way he told it?

2. From Day 2, question 6 of the workbook, have you ever identified so closely with someone in Scripture that you "imagineered" the details of that person's story and the events surrounding his or her life the way Kris did with Adam? Whom did you identify with, and what effect did putting yourself in that person's place, so to speak, have on you?

3. Kris talked in the book and the video about the possibility that "Adam" could have been both male and female before God took woman out of man. Had you ever considered that possibility before? What do you think of the concept that men and women may be two halves of a whole?

4. From today's video, Kris's introduction in the book and the materials we have gone over so far, you may already have a sense about whether your views on the role of women will align very closely with Kris's views, somewhat closely, or be very far apart. Whatever the case, why would it be a good thing to see this study through to the end?

Life Application Check (10 minutes): Many participants leave a group study feeling that the teaching was insightful, the discussion lively and the meeting a success. But they also leave feeling that one important question went unanswered: "What do I do *next* to apply the principles I learned to my life and my spiritual walk?" To prevent that, I have included a "Life Application" section in every session of the participant workbook. Each application directs the participants to *do something* in response to what they learned through their study of the principles in that particular session. During your group meeting, it would be beneficial to spend a few minutes going over the "Life Application" section. Read the application aloud from the workbook and allow time for a couple testimonies of what group members did in response and what good things resulted from their efforts to apply this session to their lives.

If some participants have not done the application, urge them to go back and try it as soon as possible in the coming week. This is an important part of any study. It really brings the lessons home and helps people apply what they are learning to daily life. There would be little point in studying *Fashioned to Reign* at all if it had a net effect of zero on your life or ministry!

Closing Prayer/Ministry (time will vary): Make any announcements your group will need to be aware of before the next meeting. Make sure to include a mention of which workbook session your participants should work through in preparation for next time. (In this case, they should work through Session 2 in preparation for the next meeting.) Encourage everyone again to participate fully in the study by doing the five daily workbook sections and the readings that go along with those, so that they get the most out of the material. Then offer a closing prayer to wrap up your meeting, or ask someone in the group to do so, and dismiss the group members to return home.

Usually by the time you move through your meeting schedule and get to the closing prayer, some people will need to leave. If there are those present who desire prayer for anything specific, however, you could invite them to stay, if time allows, so that leadership can minister to them.

If the members of your group are not pressed for time by work schedules or family responsibilities, think about making this ministry time a regular element at the close of your meetings. Check ahead about whether your meeting place would allow for the group to stay a little longer, and then invite those who wish to stay to take part in prayer and ministry together after your meetings. This will give the Holy Spirit room to move in people's lives in response to the lessons they have learned. It is also a good way to take the life application practice even further, and it can provide a sweet and powerful conclusion to your meetings.

Session 2 Guide

Unmasking the Devil

*I*n brief, Session 2 covers material from chapter 3 of *Fashioned to Reign*, along with the Session 2 pages from the participant workbook. In this session, we unmask the masked serpent as I present some Scriptures that tell us more about the history of Lucifer prior to the creation story. I look at how he weaseled his way into the life of the first family and tempted Eve, and through her tempted Adam, to change masters. The consequences of that momentous decision fell on them all as God pronounced a curse first on the serpent, then on the man and woman. But God also promised Adam and Eve and all of humankind redemption from the curse in the form of Jesus Christ, our Savior. Have both men *and* women received the fullness of that redemption? That is the important question we close with at the end of this session. I also talk about the famous warrior and martyr Joan of Arc, who knew her Lord and Master and fearlessly went forth in His name.

Leadership Prayer Focus (before the meeting): Ask the Lord to give your participants clear insight into who the devil is and why he harbors such enmity against women. Pray that they will understand the fullness of redemption offered through Jesus Christ to both men *and* women, a redemption that brings freedom from every curse and consequence of the Fall.

Welcome and Fellowship Time (20–30 minutes): Be ready 20 minutes before your meeting to start welcoming participants. Connect with each person as he or she arrives. Direct people to enjoy some fellowship (and refreshments if applicable) until the group begins. Check with any new participants about whether they have a *Fashioned to Reign* book and workbook, and help them get hold of the materials if needed. Ideally, participants will have worked through Session 2 by now, which is the material you will cover in this meeting.

Gather and Begin (10 minutes): Gather everyone together, along with their books, workbooks and something to write with. Introduce yourself and briefly outline the purpose of the group—to study *Fashioned to Reign* together and learn about the way God fashioned, called and equipped women to co-reign alongside men.

If you wish, allow participants to again give their names and perhaps one interesting fact about themselves, as they did at the first meeting. Briefly overview what the coming sessions will look like, and mention again that you will cover one workbook session per meeting and that participants should read the materials and do the workbook pages for that session *prior* to the meetings.

This might be a good time to ask your group members how their daily study time in preparation for the meetings has gone for these first two sessions. Encourage them to continue fully engaging with the curriculum to get the most out of this study. Also, if you are including an optional ninth session, remind the group again about that final meeting being dedicated to wrap-up and fellowship.

Opening Prayer, Worship (10 minutes): Pray for the meeting aloud, or ask a group member to do so. If your group includes worship, enter into that now to prepare your hearts to receive whatever the Holy Spirit has for you in this meeting. Remember as group leader to put in place ahead of time your method for worship and double-check AV equipment so that it functions properly. Be alert in this time of worship since people may receive words of knowledge, wisdom or prophetic words.

It is easy to get lost in worship, so remember that it is up to you to steward your participants' time well and monitor the group for distractions. Once you sense that the Holy Spirit is ready for you to move on into the study portion of your meeting, help the group make that transition. Gently direct those who might monopolize the group's time with personal problems or issues to put their comments on hold and talk to you after the group meeting is concluded. At that time, you can minister to them on a deeper level or direct them to an appropriate counselor in the church who can help them further.

Video Teaching (20–30 minutes): At this point, transition into teaching time by having the group watch the video segment that goes along with Session 2. Participants should have workbooks and pens in hand so they can fill in the video guide in the workbook as they watch and listen. The video segment will give them all the information they need to fill in the blanks, and you will review the answers with them after the video. Again, make sure to test all AV equipment *prior* to your meeting so that when you push *PLAY*, the video plays!

Here are the answers for the Session 2 video guide. Review these answers with your group after the video so they can fill in any blanks they missed.

1. The word *enmity* is translated from the Hebrew word for <u>hostility</u>.

2. The curse over the <u>serpent</u> is that woman will be <u>hostile</u> toward him.

3. When you think about that curse, it makes sense that almost all <u>spiritual</u> <u>warfare</u> is directed at <u>women</u>.

4. The spear point of spiritual warfare is women. Every religion figures out some way to <u>reduce</u> women. Every culture figures out some way to <u>reduce</u> women.

5. The curse over the woman is that your <u>husband</u> will rule over you. God did not take <u>men</u> and put them over women.

6. Before the curse, Adam and Eve <u>co-reigned</u>.

7. Relationally, Adam needed the <u>woman</u> to make him <u>complete</u> because the woman was <u>taken</u> <u>out</u> of the man.

8. Eve was a <u>brilliant</u> woman whom the serpent and Adam both <u>listened</u> to and were both <u>influenced</u> by.

9. Jesus became the curse, and so there is no curse that's <u>valid</u> or <u>appropriate</u> anymore.

10. A curse means you can do the <u>right</u> <u>thing</u>, but the <u>wrong</u> <u>thing</u> still happens. Jesus became a curse so that we could become <u>free</u> from the curse.

11. When Jesus died on the cross, He <u>broke</u> the <u>curse</u>.

12. When God restores, He restores people to a <u>better</u> <u>place</u> than they began. God doesn't say let Me fix you; He says let Me <u>re-create</u> you (see 2 Corinthians 5:17).

Discussion/Dialogue Time (30–40 minutes): Now it is time for your group members to dialogue about the things they are learning. Open up the dialogue with the following discussion questions. Some questions are new, from the fresh ideas I presented in the video segment. Others revisit some of the questions I asked in the daily workbook pages for this session, so that participants have a chance to talk over their workbook answers and gain insight from each other. If there are Scriptures connected to a particular question, encourage participation by asking a group member to read the Scripture aloud. Then read the discussion question to the group and ask for input.

Session 2 Discussion Questions

1. Kris said in today's video that until he wrote *Fashioned to Reign*, he did not really understand that the curse over the *serpent* was that God would put enmity or hostility between him and the woman. How does that explain in part why the devil is so threatened by the possibility of women coming into their full destiny?

2. In both the book and the video, Kris mentions a number of ways in which Eve was both powerful and influential in the Garden. How does this differ from many Christians' views of her? Why does it differ from our view of her?

3. In today's video Kris asked the important question, "When do women begin to receive the Savior's full reward of the curse being broken?" From Day 4, question 1 in the workbook, how would you answer the question behind that question, "What makes us think that men were set free from the curse of the Law at the cross, but that women should still be under the curse that allows husbands to dominate them in the name of God?"

4. God restores people to a better place than they began. Rather than "fixing" fallen humanity back to the "Adam and Eve in the Garden" state, in what sense does God make anyone who is in Christ a completely new creation, something never before created?

Life Application Check (10 minutes): Now have participants answer the important question, "What do I do *next* to apply the principles I learned to my life and my spiritual walk?" Do this by going over the "Life Application" section from the workbook. Read it aloud and allow time for a couple testimonies of what group members did in response and what good things resulted from their efforts to apply this session to their lives.

If some participants have not done the applications for Sessions 1 and 2, urge them to go back and try them as soon as possible. Stress that making application is an important part of any study—possibly the most important part. Suggest that there is little point in studying spiritual principles at all if they have a net effect of zero on your life or ministry!

Closing Prayer/Ministry (time will vary): Make any necessary announcements and mention that everyone should work through Session 3 in their workbook in preparation for next time. Offer a closing prayer to wrap up your meeting, or ask someone in the group to do so, and dismiss the group members to return home.

If time and space allow and there are those present who desire prayer, invite them to stay so that leadership can minister to them. This ministry time may become a regular element at the close of your meetings. It can give the Holy Spirit room to move in people's lives in response to the lessons they have learned. It is also a good way to take the life application practice even farther, providing a powerful conclusion to your meetings.

Session 3 Guide

Standing for the Word

*I*n brief, Session 3 covers material from chapter 4 of *Fashioned to Reign*, along with the Session 3 pages from the participant workbook. In this session, I talk about the difference between *believing* every word of the Bible and *living by* every word (trying to apply all Scripture literally and universally). God wrote the Scriptures in such a way that some verses are a documentary on the way people in the Bible lived, while other verses are a commentary about God's perspective on how we are to live our lives. It is important to identify which is which. That is why we must allow Kingdom core values to guide us in the way we approach life and in the way we approach the Word. We also need to see Scripture through the lens of "Son-glasses" so that we can accurately handle the Word of Truth. It takes the Word of God *plus* the Spirit of God to equal truth and accuracy in applying the Scriptures. I also discuss how Satan tries to use the Bible as a weapon to kill, steal and destroy people's lives. Finally, we look at Harriet Tubman, the "Moses" of her people, who stood on God's unconditional love for her and let it inspire her to live out a risk-taking love for others.

Leadership Prayer Focus (before the meeting): Ask the Lord to help your participants identify the difference between *believing* every word of the Bible and trying to *live by* every word literally and universally. Pray that they would see Scripture through the correct lens, and that through this study, with the help of the Holy Spirit, they would learn how to accurately handle the Word of Truth, particularly where it concerns the empowerment of women.

Welcome and Fellowship Time (20–30 minutes): Be ready 20 minutes before your meeting to start welcoming participants. Connect with each person as he or she arrives. Direct people to enjoy some fellowship (and refreshments if applicable) until the group begins. Check with any new participants about whether they have a *Fashioned to Reign* book and workbook, and help them get hold of the materials if needed. Ideally, participants will have worked through Session 3 by now, which is the material you will cover in this meeting.

Gather and Begin (10 minutes): Gather everyone together, along with their books, workbooks and something to write with. Introduce yourself and briefly outline the purpose of the group—to study *Fashioned to Reign* together and learn about the way God fashioned, called and equipped women to co-reign alongside men.

If you wish, allow participants to again give their names and perhaps one interesting fact about themselves, as they did at the first meeting. Briefly overview what the coming sessions will look like, and mention again that you will cover one session per meeting and that participants should read the materials and do the workbook pages for that session *prior* to the meetings. Encourage everyone to continue fully engaging with the curriculum to get the most out of this study.

Opening Prayer, Worship (10 minutes): Pray for the meeting aloud, or ask a group member to do so. If your group includes worship, enter into that now to prepare your hearts to receive whatever the Holy Spirit has for you in this meeting. Remember as group leader to put in place ahead of time your method for worship and double-check AV equipment so that it functions properly. Be alert in this time of worship since people may receive words of knowledge, wisdom or prophetic words.

Steward your participants' time well. Once you sense that the Holy Spirit is ready for you to move on into the study portion of your meeting, help the group make that transition. As before, gently direct those who might monopolize the group's time with personal problems to put their comments on hold and talk to you after the meeting. At that time, minister to them on a deeper level or direct them to an appropriate counselor in the church.

Video Teaching (20–30 minutes): At this point, transition into teaching time by having the group watch the video segment that goes along with Session 3. Participants should have workbooks and pens in hand so they can fill in the video guide in the workbook as they watch and listen. Again, make sure to test all AV equipment *prior* to your meeting.

Here are the answers for the Session 3 video guide. Review these answers with your group after the video so they can fill in any blanks they missed.

1. The <u>letter</u> kills, but the <u>Spirit</u> gives life (see 2 Corinthians 3:6).

2. The Word of God in the hands of the <u>devil</u> is not <u>true</u>.

3. It takes the Word of God and the <u>Spirit</u> to make truth.

4. Proverbs shows what happens when the <u>wisest</u> man in the world has a <u>relationship</u> with God. Ecclesiastes shows what happens when the <u>wisest</u> man in the world <u>loses</u> relationship with God.

5. The <u>application</u> of the Word of God needs to be <u>directed</u> by the Holy Spirit.

6. The Spirit of God <u>leads</u> us into <u>all truth</u>.

7. You <u>process</u> the Bible through the <u>lens</u> of the Holy Spirit.

8. Truth is held in <u>tension</u>.

9. Some of the Bible is a <u>documentary</u>, and some of the Bible is a <u>commentary</u>. Sometimes God is telling us a <u>story</u>; other times, God is saying, "This is how it should happen."

10. Millions and millions of Christian women have been <u>oppressed</u> because people have taken a documentary and they've <u>made</u> it a commentary.

Discussion/Dialogue Time (30–40 minutes): Now it is time for your group members to dialogue about the things they are learning. Open up the dialogue with the following discussion questions. If there are Scriptures connected to a particular question, encourage participation by asking a group member to read the Scripture aloud. Then read the discussion question to the group and ask for input.

—— *Session 3 Discussion Questions* ——

1. Kris gave the striking (and imaginary) example in today's video of a parent sending his sixteen-year-old son to a Christian counselor because of a problem with pornography and having the young man come home missing one eye and one hand because of a literal application of the Scriptures. Why is it so easy for us to see that that kind of application is wrong, yet so hard for us to make less obvious distinctions from Scripture? How might knowing the "back story" of a Scripture make a difference?

2. From Day 2, question 1 in the workbook, what does Kris mean when he says there is "truth held in tension" between different Scriptures?

3. In both the book and the video, Kris emphasized the huge difference between scriptural *documentary* and scriptural *commentary*. How does that relate to the difference between believing every word of the Bible and living every word? Are we even meant to live every word of it?

4. From the video and Day 3, question 2 in the workbook, how did the question of slavery in the American Civil War illustrate the deadly ramifications of confusing God's narratives in Scripture with God's commands? Additionally, how might it make sense that the issue of empowering women in the Church today is the result of similar confusion?

Life Application Check (10 minutes): Now have participants answer the important question, "What do I do *next* to apply the principles I learned to my life and my spiritual walk?" Do this by going over the "Life Application" section from the workbook. Read it aloud and allow time for a couple testimonies of what group members did in response and what good things resulted from their efforts to apply this session to their lives.

If some participants have not done the applications for these early sessions, have them go back and try them. Stress again that application is an important part of any study—possibly the most important part.

Closing Prayer/Ministry (time will vary): Make any necessary announcements and mention that everyone should work through Session 4 in their workbook in preparation for next time. Offer a closing prayer to wrap up your meeting, or ask someone in the group to do so, and dismiss the group members to return home.

If time and space allow and there are those present who desire prayer, invite them to stay so that leadership can minister to them. This ministry time can give the Holy Spirit room to move in people's lives in response to the lessons they have learned, and it can provide a powerful conclusion to your meetings.

Session 4 Guide

The First Women's Lib Movement

*I*n brief, Session 4 covers material from chapter 5 of *Fashioned to Reign*, along with the Session 4 pages from the participant workbook. Jesus was the founder of the first women's liberation movement, and this session takes a look at why I make that claim. First-century Jewish men had nothing in common with Jesus when it came to their mind-set toward women. Jesus talked to, taught and traveled in ministry with numerous girlfriends (meaning friends who were girls)—a radical paradigm shift from the patterns of His day. He kept some surprising female company and valued women whom His contemporaries considered of no value whatsoever. What is more, He honored His mother, Mary, and allowed her to influence His life long after He had grown into manhood. I talk about how it is possible that Jesus picked up from Mary a well of compassion for women of ill repute. He understood womanly issues and welcomed women as valuable contributors to His ministry. Women's words and stories play a major role throughout the gospels—particularly at His death and resurrection, where their track record is far better than the men who were involved in those scenarios. Finally, I take a look at Rosa Parks, who is called the Mother of the Civil Rights Movement. She exemplifies the contribution one woman can make in leading the way out of victimization into victory.

Leadership Prayer Focus (before the meeting): Ask the Lord to open the eyes of your participants to the amazing place of honor Jesus gave women and the value He placed on them in His life and ministry. Pray that any participants who struggle with having an attitude toward women in leadership would learn from His example and apply what they learn to every relationship they have with a female leader.

Welcome and Fellowship Time (20–30 minutes): Be ready 20 minutes before your meeting to start welcoming participants. Connect with each person as he or she arrives. Direct people to enjoy some fellowship (and refreshments if applicable) until the group begins. Check with any new participants about whether they have a *Fashioned to Reign* book and workbook, and help them get hold of the materials if needed. Ideally, participants will have worked through Session 4 by now, which is the material you will cover in this meeting.

Gather and Begin (10 minutes): Gather everyone together, along with their books, workbooks and something to write with. Introduce yourself and briefly outline the purpose of the group—to study *Fashioned to Reign* together and learn about the way God fashioned, called and equipped women to co-reign alongside men.

If you wish, allow participants to again give their names and perhaps one interesting fact about themselves. Briefly overview what the coming sessions will look like, and mention again that you will cover one session per meeting and that participants should read the materials and do the workbook pages for that session *prior* to the meetings. Encourage everyone to continue fully engaging with the curriculum to get the most out of this study.

Opening Prayer, Worship (10 minutes): Pray for the meeting aloud, or ask a group member to do so. If your group includes worship, enter into that now to prepare your hearts to receive whatever the Holy Spirit has for you in this meeting. Remember as group leader to put in place ahead of time your method for worship and double-check AV equipment so that it functions properly. Be alert in this time of worship since people may receive words of knowledge, wisdom or prophetic words.

Steward your participants' time well. Once you sense that the Holy Spirit is ready for you to move on into the study portion of your meeting, help the group make that transition. As before, gently direct those who might monopolize the group's time with personal problems to put their comments on hold and talk to you after the meeting. At that time, minister to them on a deeper level or direct them to an appropriate counselor in the church.

Video Teaching (20–30 minutes): At this point, transition into teaching time by having the group watch the video segment that goes along with Session 4. Participants should have workbooks and pens in hand so they can fill in the video guide in the workbook as they watch and listen. Again, make sure to test all AV equipment *prior* to your meeting.

Here are the answers for the Session 4 video guide. Review these answers with your group after the video so they can fill in any blanks they missed.

1. The Judaizers claimed <u>Moses</u> as their father, but they actually added <u>three</u> times as many laws as Moses actually gave them from God. Almost <u>one hundred</u> of those new laws were against women.

2. The curse put <u>wives</u> under <u>husbands</u>. It did not put <u>men</u> over <u>women</u>.

3. The most famous scribe of Jesus' day said, "I'd rather <u>burn</u> the Torah than <u>teach</u> it to a woman."

4. It wasn't just countercultural, it was <u>illegal</u> for Jesus to be teaching Mary (women).

5. Jesus had come to set the oppressed <u>free</u>, and there was nobody more oppressed in the days of Christ than <u>women</u>.

6. Because women were eliminated from all <u>leadership</u>, therefore the <u>passion</u> side of God was completely gone.

7. <u>Weeping</u> was women's work; men did not <u>weep</u>. But Jesus weeps because He is saying to Mary and to women everywhere, "I get you. I connect with you. I <u>understand</u> you."

8. The world is so absent of the <u>passionate</u>, <u>emotional</u>, <u>intelligent</u> side of God because we have left women out of our culture and oppressed them.

Discussion/Dialogue Time (30–40 minutes): Now it is time for your group members to dialogue about the things they are learning. Open up the dialogue with the following discussion questions. If there are Scriptures connected to a particular question, encourage participation by asking a group member to read the Scripture aloud. Then read the discussion question to the group and ask for input.

—— *Session 4 Discussion Questions* ——

1. In today's video, Kris mentioned how powerful some of the women of the Old Testament were (Deborah the prophetess and judge, Miriam the prophetess and some of the queens) and pointed out that God had positive things to say about their leadership. What happened in the four hundred years between the book of Malachi and the book of Matthew that caused Jesus to enter into a Jewish culture that completely banned women from any form of leadership? What did He do about it?

2. From Day 2, question 3 in the workbook, how does being familiar with the situation women faced in the first century help us understand Jesus' interactions with them?

3. Kris told the story in the video about how three times in the gospels, women broke into Jesus' private meetings, got down on the ground and began to kiss His feet. Rather than rebuking them, Jesus commended them. What do you think it was about the way these women "lived out loud" that Jesus liked? What does that mean for us as His Church?

4. In Day 4, question 3 of the workbook, Kris noted that Jesus chose not to promote any of His female disciples into the position of one of His twelve apostles and asked if the book's explanation of why Jesus did that made sense to you. What was your answer, and do you think Jesus would still need to make the same choice today? Why or why not?

5. In the prayer time at the end of the video, Kris said that we need to liberate women not to become feminists, but to become feminine. What does that mean in light of Jesus being the first women's libber, so to speak?

Life Application Check (10 minutes): Now have participants answer the important question, "What do I do *next* to apply the principles I learned to my life and my spiritual walk?" Do this by going over the "Life Application" section from the workbook. Read it aloud and allow time for a couple testimonies of what group members did in response and what good things resulted from their efforts to apply this session to their lives.

In another of my books, *Spirit Wars* (Chosen, 2012), I include a section about how important it is to steward our testimonies. We put a high priority on doing that at Bethel Church, and we continue to see the fruits of it. This might be a good time to appoint someone in the group to write down the testimonies that come forth in your group conversations from this meeting onward. At each session, have that person come prepared to note down the testimonies in a special place. In your final meeting several sessions ahead, consider encouraging everyone by reading some of these testimonies back as part of your group wrap-up or conclusion celebration.

If some participants have not done the applications for these early sessions, have them go back and try them. Stress again that application is an important part of any study—possibly the most important part.

Closing Prayer/Ministry (time will vary): Make any necessary announcements and mention that everyone should work through Session 5 in their workbook in preparation for next time. Offer a closing prayer to wrap up your meeting, or ask someone in the group to do so, and dismiss the group members to return home.

If time and space allow and there are those present who desire prayer, invite them to stay so that leadership can minister to them. This ministry time can give the Holy Spirit room to move in people's lives in response to the lessons they have learned, providing a powerful conclusion to your meetings.

Session 5 Guide

Just a Misunderstanding

*I*n brief, Session 5 covers material from chapter 6 of *Fashioned to Reign*, along with the Session 5 pages from the participant workbook. This session is all about a misunderstanding—or more than one, really. We misunderstand the apostle Paul's perspective on women. We misunderstand the cultures that Paul addressed in his epistles that "restrict" women in the Church. We misunderstand their cultural issues, which caused so many issues for the churches. We misunderstand which churches Paul was writing to and why. And we misunderstand his use of some very important terms, translating them numerous ways from the Greek, but not necessarily accurately. By process of elimination, I take a look at what Paul's restrictive passages *cannot* mean, which gives us some clues about what they do mean. When all is said and done, it turns out that for a first-century Jewish male who was also a former Pharisee, Paul was a strikingly powerful promoter of women. I think he would have appreciated the lady we take a look at as we conclude this session, the profound and practical preacher and teacher, Joyce Meyer.

Leadership Prayer Focus (before the meeting): Ask the Lord to clear up through this session any misunderstandings your participants may have regarding the "restrictions" Paul seemingly placed on women in the Church. Ask that their minds will be sharpened as you discuss various passages and their differing translations. Pray that each person in the group, male and female, will understand the profound implications a correct interpretation of Paul's writings has for women leaders in the Church.

Welcome and Fellowship Time (20–30 minutes): Be ready 20 minutes before your meeting to start welcoming participants. Connect with each person as he or she arrives. Direct people to enjoy some fellowship (and refreshments if applicable) until the group begins. Check with any new participants about whether they have a *Fashioned to Reign* book and workbook, and help them get hold of the materials if needed. Ideally, participants will have worked through Session 5 by now, which is the material you will cover in this meeting.

Gather and Begin (10 minutes): Gather everyone together, along with their books, workbooks and something to write with. Introduce yourself and briefly outline the purpose of the group—to study *Fashioned to Reign* together and learn about the way God fashioned, called and equipped women to co-reign alongside men.

If you wish, allow participants to again give their names and perhaps one interesting fact about themselves. Briefly overview what the remaining sessions will look like, and mention again that you will cover one session per meeting and that participants should read the materials and do the workbook pages for that session *prior* to the meetings. Encourage everyone to continue fully engaging with the curriculum to get the most out of this study.

Opening Prayer, Worship (10 minutes): Pray for the meeting aloud, or ask a group member to do so. If your group includes worship, enter into that now to prepare your hearts to receive whatever the Holy Spirit has for you in this meeting. Remember as group leader to put in place ahead of time your method for worship and double-check AV equipment. Be alert in this time of worship since people may receive words of knowledge, wisdom or prophetic words.

Steward your participants' time well. Once you sense that the Holy Spirit is ready for you to move on into the study portion of your meeting, help the group make that transition. As before, gently direct those who might monopolize the group's time with personal problems to put their comments on hold and talk to you after the meeting. At that time, minister to them on a deeper level or direct them to an appropriate counselor in the church.

Video Teaching (20–30 minutes): At this point, transition into teaching time by having the group watch the video segment that goes along with Session 5. Participants should have workbooks and pens in hand so they can fill in the video guide in the workbook as they watch and listen. Again, make sure to test all AV equipment *prior* to your meeting.

Here are the answers for the Session 5 video guide. Review these answers with your group after the video so they can fill in any blanks they missed.

1. Most of the <u>restrictions</u> (on women) that we hear about in church and in the Bible come from an apostle who is actually very <u>empowering</u>.

2. We all (as Christians) believe in the Bible; the question is, how do we actually <u>apply</u> the Bible? It is important not just to know the

Word of God, but to know how to apply the right <u>word</u> in the right <u>season</u>.

3. Paul wrote <u>thirteen</u> books of the Bible to <u>nine</u> different cities.

4. When we're talking about the epistles, the letters written to different churches, we're taking about letters written to churches in three separate cultures—the <u>Jewish</u> culture, the <u>Roman</u> culture and the <u>Greek</u> culture.

5. The Greeks believed that women were more <u>powerful</u> than men, and so they made <u>gods</u> out of women.

6. The only culture Paul wrote anything to that could even seemingly be <u>restrictive</u> was the <u>Greek</u> culture.

7. The epistles were letters written to <u>specific</u> cities about <u>specific</u> issues.

8. You can't <u>universally</u> apply a letter written to a specific person about a specific problem.

9. You use <u>authority</u> to give it away, not to <u>keep</u> it.

10. Pray that God would release us from the <u>religious</u> <u>spirit</u> that uses the <u>Bible</u> to oppress people.

Discussion/Dialogue Time (30–40 minutes): Now allow time for your group members to dialogue about the things they are learning. Open up the dialogue with the following discussion questions. If there are Scriptures connected to a particular question, encourage participation by asking a group member to read the Scripture aloud. Then read the discussion question to the group and ask for input.

—— *Session 5 Discussion Questions* ——————

1. Kris pointed out in today's video and the book that of the nine different cities Paul addressed in his epistles, only to the places with Greek culture did he write anything restrictive about women. Given that the Jewish and Roman cultures oppressed women, but the Greek culture made them temple prostitutes/priestesses and goddesses, why does that make sense?

2. From Day 2, question 1, now that we are five sessions into this study, what kind of response are you having to it? And is your response

to the empowerment of women based on the teachings or opinions of others? How is this study helping you explore for yourself the scriptural evidence for the empowerment of female believers?

3. How does knowing about Paul's format of repeating and answering questions as he wrote the book of Corinthians affect your interpretation of his "restrictive" verses on women? Does knowing about the "No way!" (ἤ) symbol he liked to use for emphasis shed any light on Paul's comments for you?

4. From Day 5, question 4, in what ways has it become clear to you that Paul, even though he was a first-century Jewish male and a former Pharisee, was also a shockingly powerful promoter of women?

Life Application Check (10 minutes): Now have participants answer the important question, "What do I do *next* to apply the principles I learned to my life and my spiritual walk?" Do this by going over the "Life Application" section from the workbook. Read it aloud and allow time for a couple testimonies of what group members did in response and what good things resulted from their efforts to apply this session to their lives.

If some participants have not done the applications for any sessions, have them go back and try them. Stress again that application is an important part of any study—possibly the most important part.

Closing Prayer/Ministry (time will vary): Make any necessary announcements and mention that everyone should work through Session 6 in their workbook in preparation for next time. Offer a closing prayer to wrap up your meeting, or ask someone in the group to do so, and dismiss the group members to return home.

If time and space allow and there are those present who desire prayer, invite them to stay so that leadership can minister to them. This ministry time can give the Holy Spirit room to move in people's lives in response to the lessons they have learned, providing a powerful conclusion to your meetings.

Session 6 Guide

A Careful Excavation

*I*n brief, Session 6 covers material from chapter 7 of *Fashioned to Reign*, along with the Session 6 pages from the participant workbook. This session is like an archaeological dig in which we excavate the sites of Paul's "restrictive" passages on women right down to their foundations. What I dig up along the way will change your perspective on those verses forever. The catalyst for that kind of scholarly excavation on my part was a conference I was invited to speak at in Latin America. In Days 1 and 2 of this session, I talk about that experience and relate the vision God gave me as I traveled and prepared to speak. It was a vision of tsunamis and storms versus scepters and thrones, a vision of Satan's plan versus God's plan for the women of the Church there (and everywhere) to rise up and rule and reign alongside men. At the conclusion of this session, we look at a woman who did just that in a most amazing way—Aimee Semple McPherson, founder of the Foursquare Fellowship.

Leadership Prayer Focus (before the meeting): Ask the Lord to continue bringing clarity to the minds of your participants as you continue to excavate more scriptural passages regarding women. Pray that any shaky foundations on which participants have built their beliefs about women in leadership would be rebuilt and repaired with the solid scriptural building blocks presented in this session.

Welcome and Fellowship Time (20–30 minutes): Be ready 20 minutes before your meeting to start welcoming participants. Connect with each person as he or she arrives. Direct people to enjoy some fellowship (and refreshments if applicable) until the group begins. Check with any new participants about whether they have a *Fashioned to Reign* book and workbook, and help them get hold of the materials if needed. Ideally, participants will have worked through Session 6 by now, which is the material you will cover in this meeting.

Gather and Begin (10 minutes): Gather everyone together, along with their books, workbooks and something to write with. Introduce yourself and briefly outline the purpose of the group—to study *Fashioned to Reign* together and learn about the way God fashioned, called and equipped women to co-reign alongside men.

If you wish, allow participants to again give their names and perhaps one interesting fact about themselves. Briefly overview what the remaining sessions will look like, and mention again that you will cover one session per meeting and that participants should read the materials and do the workbook pages for that session *prior* to the meetings. Encourage everyone to continue fully engaging with the curriculum to get the most out of this study.

Opening Prayer, Worship (10 minutes): Pray for the meeting aloud, or ask a group member to do so. If your group includes worship, enter into that now to prepare your hearts to receive whatever the Holy Spirit has for you in this meeting. Remember as group leader to put in place ahead of time your method for worship and double-check AV equipment. Be alert in this time of worship since people may receive words of knowledge, wisdom or prophetic words.

Steward your participants' time well. Once you sense that the Holy Spirit is ready for you to move on into the study portion of your meeting, help the group make that transition. As before, gently direct those who might monopolize the group's time with personal problems to put their comments on hold and talk to you after the meeting. At that time, minister to them on a deeper level or direct them to an appropriate counselor in the church.

Video Teaching (20–30 minutes): At this point, transition into teaching time by having the group watch the video segment that goes along with Session 6. Participants should have workbooks and pens in hand so they can fill in the video guide in the workbook as they watch and listen. Again, make sure to test all AV equipment *prior* to your meeting.

Here are the answers for the Session 6 video guide. Review these answers with your group after the video so they can fill in any blanks they missed.

1. The New Testament ought to be more <u>empowering</u> than the Old Testament where all of us lived under a <u>curse</u>.

2. Sometimes people do not want to look at the <u>context</u> of a Scripture because it violates their understanding of what should happen in their <u>churches</u>.

3. Women <u>taught</u> in Bible days, for example <u>Priscilla</u> with her husband, Aquila, in Acts 18:26.

4. <u>Authority</u> means to <u>slap</u> with the back of a hand in 1 Timothy 2.

5. Women and men were <u>created</u> to rule and reign <u>together</u>.

6. God never intended to <u>belittle</u> women or to make them "<u>less</u> <u>than</u>."

7. You cannot apply the epistles the way you would an Old Testament book because the epistles were written to specific <u>people</u> to cover specific <u>issues</u> at specific <u>times</u>.

Discussion/Dialogue Time (30–40 minutes): Now allow time for your group members to dialogue about the things they are learning. Open up the dialogue with the following discussion questions. If there are Scriptures connected to a particular question, encourage participation by asking a group member to read the Scripture aloud. Then read the discussion question to the group and ask for input.

—— *Session 6 Discussion Questions* ——

1. Kris said in today's video that he has found that it is not so much that male leadership in the churches *want* to use the Bible to oppress women. Rather, they want to honor God by making sure they are not applying Scripture in unintended ways just because it suits them or "feels right." While that has probably slowed down the empowerment of women in some places, what is the positive side of that attitude of the heart?

2. Kris detailed in both the book and the video the difficulties he faced in dialoging with male leadership who initially opposed what he had to say about the empowerment of women in the Church. From Day 1, question 4, do you think that after completing this study, you may need to share what you have learned about the empowerment of women in God's Kingdom with some who may not receive it very well? What will you do to make sure you are not argumentative with them, but rather, will speak the truth in love, as Kris did?

3. In the dream or vision Kris spoke about, what did the two different-colored scepters and the side-by-side thrones represent? What were the men saying to the women when they handed them a scepter and

invited them to be seated on a throne? What might those actions on the part of men look like in actual, everyday life?

4. From Day 4, question 4, what do you think it takes to both glean wisdom from the whole of Paul's epistles and to avoid misapplying these important passages of Scripture regarding the role of women in the Church?

Life Application Check (10 minutes): Now have participants answer the important question, "What do I do *next* to apply the principles I learned to my life and my spiritual walk?" Do this by going over the "Life Application" section from the workbook. Read it aloud and allow time for a couple testimonies of what group members did in response and what good things resulted from their efforts to apply this session to their lives.

If some participants have not done the applications for any sessions, have them go back and try them. Stress again that application is an important part of any study—possibly the most important part.

Closing Prayer/Ministry (time will vary): Make any necessary announcements and mention that everyone should work through Session 7 in their workbook in preparation for next time. Offer a closing prayer to wrap up your meeting, or ask someone in the group to do so, and dismiss the group members to return home.

If time and space allow and there are those present who desire prayer, invite them to stay so that leadership can minister to them. This ministry time can give the Holy Spirit room to move in people's lives in response to the lessons they have learned, providing a powerful conclusion to your meetings.

Session 7 Guide

Role Reversals

*I*n brief, Session 7 covers material from chapter 8 of *Fashioned to Reign*, along with the Session 7 pages from the participant workbook. In this session, I explore one of the unique social dynamics at work in our world today—how the absence of women taking their proper place in society has caused men to try to fulfill both masculine and feminine roles. I talk about gender differences and how they should be acknowledged, but should not be used to create inequality. I also talk about the "G.I. Jane" syndrome and the lie that men and women are the same. Similarly, I expose the false idea that gender equals personality type, when in reality the two are completely separate concepts. On a lighter note, I tell you in this session how Kathy uses the word *ah* to express several different meanings, and I relate one of our conversations that it took me a long while to interpret. I know now that Kathy's *ahs* are always full of that instinctual insight women have—a fact I have learned to appreciate. That took me a while, too. And finally, through the example of Sarah Edwards, we discover that a powerful woman can leave a world-changing legacy through her lineage.

Leadership Prayer Focus (before the meeting): Ask the Lord that He would reveal to your participants any role reversals or role confusion that they need to address in their lives. Pray that any "G.I. Janes" among your female participants would determine whether they became a G.I. Jane by design, because of who God created them to be, or whether they became a G.I. Jane because of their reaction to a dysfunctional situation. Pray that any "Sleeping Beauties" among the ladies in the group would feel the kiss of their Prince awakening them to step into their destinies as powerful women of God.

Welcome and Fellowship Time (20–30 minutes): Be ready 20 minutes before your meeting to start welcoming participants. Connect with each person as he or she arrives. Direct people to enjoy some fellowship (and refreshments if applicable) until the group begins. Check with any new participants about whether they have a *Fashioned to Reign* book and workbook, and help them get hold of the materials if needed. (Since you are nearing the conclusion of your study, suggest that any newcomers sign up for an upcoming *Fashioned to Reign* group, if one will be available. If not, they can still benefit from going back and studying the book and workbook individually.) Ideally, participants will have worked through Session 7 by now, which is the material you will cover in this meeting.

Gather and Begin (10 minutes): Gather everyone together, along with their books, workbooks and something to write with. Introduce yourself and briefly outline the purpose of the group—to study *Fashioned to Reign* together and learn about the way God fashioned, called and equipped women to co-reign alongside men.

If you wish, allow participants to again give their names and perhaps one interesting fact about themselves. Briefly overview what the remaining sessions will look like, and mention again that you will cover one session per meeting and that participants should read the materials and do the workbook pages for that session *prior* to the meetings. Encourage everyone to continue fully engaging with the curriculum to get the most out of this study.

Opening Prayer, Worship (10 minutes): Pray for the meeting aloud, or ask a group member to do so. If your group includes worship, enter into that now to prepare your hearts to receive whatever the Holy Spirit has for you in this meeting. Remember as group leader to put in place ahead of time your method for worship and double-check AV equipment. Be alert in this time of worship since people may receive words of knowledge, wisdom or prophetic words.

Steward your participants' time well. Once you sense that the Holy Spirit is ready for you to move on into the study portion of your meeting, help the group make that transition. As before, gently direct those who might monopolize the group's time with personal problems to put their comments on hold and talk to you after the meeting. At that time, minister to them on a deeper level or direct them to an appropriate counselor in the church.

Video Teaching (20–30 minutes): At this point, transition into teaching time by having the group watch the video segment that goes along with Session 7. Participants should have workbooks and pens in hand so they can fill in the video guide in the workbook as they watch and listen. Again, make sure to test all AV equipment *prior* to your meeting.

Here are the answers for the Session 7 video guide. Review these answers with your group after the video so they can fill in any blanks they missed.

1. The strength that it takes to be something you're not <u>siphons</u> off the <u>energy</u> you have to be what you are.

2. Some male leaders are <u>afraid</u> of women and don't <u>understand</u> them. You tend to <u>control</u> what you don't understand.

3. Society totally lost <u>value</u> for the <u>matriarchal</u> side of God and of women.

4. God's invisible <u>attributes</u>, His eternal <u>power</u> and divine <u>nature</u> are clearly seen in what God made.

5. God never causes us to <u>operate</u> outside of who we are. He just says, "<u>Be you</u>."

6. We're not looking for women to be <u>dominant</u> or men to be <u>dominant</u>, we're looking for <u>permission</u> to be us in any environment.

7. You'll never achieve <u>excellence</u> as a leader when you try to be somebody and something that you're <u>not</u>.

8. Women were made to lead as <u>women</u>, not as <u>men.</u>

9. You can't just marry; you have to <u>merge</u>.

10. The word *suitable* means <u>corresponding</u> to or <u>opposite</u> of.

11. If you want to make good decisions, you need the <u>patriarch</u> and the <u>matriarch</u>.

Discussion/Dialogue Time (30–40 minutes): Now allow time for your group members to dialogue about the things they are learning. Open up the dialogue with the following discussion questions. If there are Scriptures connected to a particular question, encourage participation by asking a group member to read the Scripture aloud. Then read the discussion question to the group and ask for input.

Session 7 Discussion Questions

1. In today's video, Kris asked the important question, what would happen if women and men ruled together? How might things look

different if patriarchs and matriarchs were leading equally and complementing each other according to their different strengths? Have you ever seen any examples of this in a family, church or social setting? What was the result?

2. In one of this session's book readings, Kris makes the statement that while gender distinctions should not determine *where* men and women lead, they should make a difference in *how* men and women lead. What happens when men and women are given the freedom to lead out of who they are? Why is that so vital to leading with excellence?

3. From Day 3, question 2 in the workbook, what does it mean to say that a woman processes things from the heart to the head, whereas a man processes things from the head to the heart? Can you give an example from your own experience of either processing method?

4. Kris suggested in the video that it is important for men to have the *aha* realization that they should pay close attention to a woman's *ahs*. Describe an experience you have had where that turned out to be important.

5. From Day 5, question 2, for a long time American culture has devalued the contribution and importance of mothering. Do you think that is changing? If so, what kind of changes do you see? (If you are not from America, what value does your culture place on motherhood, high or low?)

Life Application Check (10 minutes): Now have participants answer the important question, "What do I do *next* to apply the principles I learned to my life and my spiritual walk?" Do this by going over the "Life Application" section from the workbook. Read it aloud and allow time for a couple testimonies of what group members did in response and what good things resulted from their efforts to apply this session to their lives.

If some participants have not done the applications for any sessions, have them go back and try them. Stress again that application is an important part of any study—possibly the most important part.

Closing Prayer/Ministry (time will vary): Make any necessary announcements and mention that everyone should work through Session 8 in their workbook in preparation for next time. Remind everyone that Session 8 is the last meeting that will cover specific curriculum pages. If you are holding an optional ninth session to do a wrap-up or a fellowship outing, let your participants know (or decide) what that final meeting will involve. Offer a closing prayer to wrap up your meeting, or ask someone in the group to do so, and dismiss the group members to return home.

If time and space allow and there are those present who desire prayer, invite them to stay so that leadership can minister to them. This ministry time can give the Holy Spirit room to move in people's lives in response to the lessons they have learned, providing a powerful conclusion to your meetings.

Session 8 Guide

Powerful Diversity

*I*n brief, Session 8 covers material from chapter 9 and the Epilogue of *Fashioned to Reign*, along with the Session 8 pages from the participant workbook. In this session, I define what a "strong" woman is, and in many ways, the definition may surprise you. I also define the "ghost syndrome" many women battle and look at how it is triggered and how it can be dismantled through trust, honor and respect. The high value of motherhood is also a focus of this session. The significance of a woman molding the lives of her children is equal to that of a woman who runs a multimillion-dollar corporation any day. Both women are vital leaders who should be empowered to walk in their God-given identities. Paul and Peter also weigh in on marriage in this session, and we look at the Old Testament examples of Sarah and Abigail as women and wives. I touch briefly, too, on the important topic of dealing with abuse. The Gospel leaves no room for abuse in any form!

In the Epilogue, which this session also covers, I provide some answers to the question "What does it look like for a woman to be powerful?" Those answers are in the form of brief biographical descriptions of five fantastic female leaders whom I know personally. Their diversity paints a picture for you of the various dimensions of the word *powerful*. These women are one-of-a-kind inspirations who, by being themselves, exemplify the beauty and power inherent in the feminine side of God.

Leadership Prayer Focus (before the meeting): Ask the Lord to give your participants a deep and unshakable conviction about the inestimable value of women in the Kingdom of God. Ask that they also gain a new appreciation of the significance of motherhood, especially the mothers among them. Pray that any woman (or man) suffering from the "ghost syndrome" due to traumatic events of the past would find deliverance and healing through this session. Finally, ask the Lord to inspire and encourage your participants through the stories of the women leaders presented in the book and through the example of any godly female leaders they may know personally.

Welcome and Fellowship Time (20–30 minutes): Be ready 20 minutes before your meeting to start welcoming participants. Connect with each person as he or she arrives. Direct people to enjoy some fellowship (and refreshments if applicable) until the group begins. Check with any new participants about whether they have a *Fashioned to Reign* book and workbook, and help them get hold of the materials if needed. (Since you are at the conclusion of your study, suggest that any newcomers sign up for an upcoming *Fashioned to Reign* group, if one will be available. If not, they can still benefit from going back and studying the book and workbook individually.) Ideally, participants will have worked through Session 8 by now, which is the material you will cover in this meeting.

Gather and Begin (10 minutes): Gather everyone together, along with their books, workbooks and something to write with. Introduce yourself and briefly outline the purpose of the group—to study *Fashioned to Reign* together and learn about the way God fashioned, called and equipped women to co-reign alongside men.

If you wish, allow participants to give their names and perhaps one interesting fact about themselves one more time. If you are holding an optional ninth session, briefly overview what that will involve. It may be a wrap-up meeting with more dialogue about points throughout this study that you all wish to return to, or perhaps it will be some kind of fellowship party or meal together to celebrate all you have learned and all the Lord has done through this study. (Your participants should now be done with the *Fashioned to Reign* book and workbook.)

Opening Prayer, Worship (10 minutes): Pray for the meeting aloud, or ask a group member to do so. If your group includes worship, enter into that now to prepare your hearts to receive whatever the Holy Spirit has for you in this meeting. Remember as group leader to put in place ahead of time your method for worship and double-check AV equipment. Be alert in this time of worship since people may receive words of knowledge, wisdom or prophetic words.

Steward your participants' time well. Once you sense that the Holy Spirit is ready for you to move on into the study portion of your meeting, help the group make that transition. As before, gently direct those who might monopolize the group's time with personal problems to put their comments on hold and talk to you after the meeting. At that time, minister to them on a deeper level or direct them to an appropriate counselor in the church.

Video Teaching (20–30 minutes): At this point, transition into teaching time by having the group watch the video segment that goes along with Session 8. Participants should have workbooks and pens in hand so they can fill in the video guide in the workbook as they watch and listen. Again, make sure to test all AV equipment *prior* to your meeting.

Here are the answers for the Session 8 video guide. Review these answers with your group after the video so they can fill in any blanks they missed.

1. Heidi Baker's strategy is just to talk to <u>Jesus</u> minute by minute.

2. Tracy Evans is the <u>bravest</u> person—not woman, but *person*—Kris knows.

3. Beni Johnson shows that there is something <u>powerful</u> about being who you want to be in Christ, not who other people want you to be.

4. When we, especially as women, know who God <u>created</u> us to be, we act out of that and we <u>minister</u> out of that.

5. The enemy always tries to <u>stifle</u> that and to tell us that we're <u>less</u> than that.

6. God showed Kathy Vallotton that to be beautiful means to be <u>you</u> until you're <u>full</u> of everything that He has placed inside you.

Discussion/Dialogue Time (30–40 minutes): Now allow time for your group members to dialogue about the things they are learning. Open up the dialogue with the following discussion questions. If there are Scriptures connected to a particular question, encourage participation by asking a group member to read the Scripture aloud. Then read the discussion question to the group and ask for input.

—— *Session 8 Discussion Questions* ——

1. Kris talked in today's video about how *powerful* does not necessarily mean being in charge of things, although it can mean that. Some powerful women lead by being in charge; some powerful women lead by being spiritual giants behind the scenes. When you think of the powerful women you know, does a diverse group come to mind, as it does for Kris? Or do you need to expand your definition of the word *powerful*?

2. Kris talked in the book and the workbook about the "ghost syndrome" and the effect it can have on people. From Day 1, question 4, have you ever experienced the ghost syndrome in yourself? Or have you ever met anyone (male or female) who seems to suffer from it? How does it interfere with effective empowerment? What are some redemptive ways you can think of that such ghosts can be put to rest?

3. Kris named Beni Johnson as a unique example of an empowered woman because she does not take on the typical "pastor's wife" roles the way other people might expect her to. How does *not* stepping into positions of leadership to meet other people's expectations show freedom and empowerment? How does it make it easier to be who you were created in Christ to be?

4. From Day 5, question 1, in your eyes, what are some of the various dimensions of the term *powerful*? How are some of the empowered women you know living examples of the feminine side of God?

Life Application Check (10 minutes): Now have participants answer the important question, "What do I do *next* to apply the principles I learned to my life and my spiritual walk?" Do this by going over the "Life Application" section from the workbook. Read it aloud and allow time for a couple testimonies of what group members did in response and what good things resulted from their efforts to apply this session to their lives.

If some participants have not done the applications for any of the previous sessions, have them commit to going back and trying them. Stress one final time that application is an important part of any study—possibly the most important part.

Closing Prayer/Ministry (time will vary): Make any necessary announcements and mention that everyone should now be finished with the *Fashioned to Reign* book and workbook. Remind everyone that this was the last meeting that covered specific book and workbook pages, but that they can go back on their own and finish any sessions or readings they missed before they conclude their personal study of this curriculum.

If this is your final meeting and time allows, this conclusion time might be a good opportunity to ask for testimonies of what God has done in the participants' lives and ministry through this study. I have mentioned how important it is to steward the testimonies, and I am sure that the stories that come forth will amaze and encourage the group. If you appointed someone back in Session 4 to steward your group's testimonies by writing them down, now would be a good time to encourage everyone by reading those testimonies back to the group. (Or include that activity as part of your wrap-up or conclusion celebration if you are having a ninth session.)

Offer a closing prayer to wrap up your meeting, or ask someone in the group to do so, and dismiss the group members to return home. If there are still those present who desire prayer, invite them to stay so that leadership can minister to them. Make sure as leader that even though your group meetings are at an end, anyone who needs additional counsel has been connected with someone in your group or church who can move them forward in their understanding of the role of empowered women in the Church.

If you are holding an optional ninth session to do a wrap-up or fellowship outing, let your participants know what that final meeting will involve for next time. Make sure everyone knows where and when that meeting will take place, if different from your usual meeting site, day or time. You may want to invite your participants to come ready with their testimonies of what God has done through this study, so that you can celebrate their testimonies at that final meeting. (If your group has been keeping a written record of the testimonies, you can use it at that meeting to encourage everyone.)

Optional Final Meeting

Fashioned to Reign Celebration

This final session is optional. Your group participants should all be finished with the *Fashioned to Reign* curriculum. In the first eight sessions the book has been read, the workbook has been filled out, the videos have been viewed and the questions have been discussed, so you do not have any curriculum to cover at this meeting. Yet perhaps your group is not ready to disband or move on without some sort of wrap-up to the time you have spent together, learning about the God-ordained role of beautiful and powerful women in the Church and in the earth. If you feel your group would benefit from a final session to finish processing the materials, or if your participants want to come back to some points and finish discussing them in more depth, this would be an ideal time to set aside for that kind of wrap-up.

Or what about having a celebration together? As a group, you may decide to hold more of a celebration/fellowship for this optional conclusion meeting. Perhaps you will want to share a meal together, along with sharing new or already recorded testimonies of what the Holy Spirit has accomplished in your lives through this *Fashioned to Reign* study.

To make this ninth and final session memorable, you could choose from several options. The group as a whole could meet at a local restaurant as a special activity, or you could hold a dinner at someone's home. There may even be a few culinary artists among you who would love to prepare a celebratory meal for the group. Or you could arrange a potluck where everyone contributes to the meal.

Whatever method you choose to wrap up your *Fashioned to Reign* study, make it a celebration. Your group has come a long way together, covering a lot of scriptural and spiritual territory in new depth as you excavated to the very foundations your beliefs about the role of women in the Church. You all have become equipped with a clearer understanding of the way men and women were created to complement and complete each other as both genders work together to bring healing to an ailing world and to fulfill the Great Commission.

As all of you, both men and women, walk together in the fullness of your God-given destinies, remember the things I have said in the pages of *Fashioned to Reign* about our mandate and mission of encouraging women to live powerfully. Read these words from the book to your group as a final exhortation:

> The truths we have learned here will become our drawbridge over the dangerous moat of religion that encircles the walls of the evil fortress of deception. These truths will become the thick climbing rope we will use to scale the castle tower of tradition and the sharp, double-edged sword we will wield to defeat the enemy. Our ultimate mission is to rescue God's princesses from decades of captivity and powerlessness, and to restore them to their rightful throne next to their King.